IN URGENT PURSUIT

OF

Hope

*My Journey from Codependent Captivity to a Life
Full of Favor and Freedom!*

SHERYL M. KRAFT

I have tried to recreate events, locales and conversations from my memories of them. In order to maintain their anonymity in some instances I have changed the names of individuals and places. I also may have changed some identifying characteristics and details such as physical properties, occupations and places of residence.

 Dedication

This book is dedicated to everyone who has walked or is still walking through any form of heartache, brokenness, or tragedy; yet is determined to not allow it to define them or their future. My prayer is that through my story, you will find strong encouragement to forgive, grow, hope, dream, and to love again. With God, ALL things are possible!

Acknowledgements

One of the many life lessons that I have learned, especially within the past three years, is to daily remain teachable and thankful.

To You, Jesus, I owe You my life. You would never let me out of Your sight or Your loving arms even when I was in my darkest moments. Thank You God, for all of the divine appointments (people, angels, and events) that You have strategically placed in my journey to encourage me and to point me towards my destiny.

To my amazing counselors, Debbie and Katy, thank you for your tough love as you walked me through acknowledging painful truth, so I could heal, grow and continue to move forward in God's calling upon my life.

To my parents, sister and extended family for never giving up on me and for always being there to love, encourage, support and pray for me day and night whenever I needed you. I love you all ferociously!

To my true friends all over the globe who knew the truth, knew my heart, and who never gave up encouraging and praying for me to keep my eyes fixed upon Jesus no matter what.

To many of the Elijahlist prophetic ministers of the Gospel and other prophetic apostles that I am aligned with, oh how I thank God for you and your timely prophetic words. Holy Spirit was constantly confirming, encouraging, instructing and drawing me deeper still through them all.

To my little furry bundle of joy, Chay Chay, you have truly been my little gift from God for the past 10 years now. You have always been so very attentive to my emotional needs for unconditional love, comfort and companionship. You have surpassed living up to your Hebrew name of (a double portion of) life, revival and renewal.

Contents

Foreword

BY KELLEY GOODALL

In the years I have listened to and supported the hearts and minds of people who are struggling to receive healing and to change and grow from the adversities that have captured them, I have observed many responses from each person in their efforts to come into promised victory.

When I met Sheryl, she was a meek and very broken woman. She had a true ideal of who she wanted to be and what her life and relationships with others and God should look like. However, she learned that little of what she expected was her reality. What she did not know was how to get to the complete fulfillment she longed for, what it would cost her to do so, or how long the journey would take.

This, I believe, is true in some measure for each of us. I also believe it is part of the majesty of the Lord in His divine plan for us to encounter and discover Him in His fullness and ascertain who we are in Him as He made us each in His likeness, with our own delightful uniqueness.

This book is a compilation of Sheryl's unearthing of the person, the individual, the woman that God created for her to become as well as to be each day, i.e., with herself and with each person she encounters including her Holy God. Through her journey, she sought hard and listened deeply to the Spirit of the Lord as He guided her through countless challenges, hurts, disappointments, struggles and pain. Along the way, she established and confirmed the foundations of her beliefs and values. She intentionally engaged in seeking the Lord and followed the steps He defined for her. In doing so, her path of healing began to transpire and with it came beautiful changes.

Transformation occurred within her and around her as a result of her obedience to the Lord's directives (Rom 12:1-2). Sometimes she wondered or questioned what she was to do or how to get the things done that He revealed to her, but her faith and persistence carried her through and were vital to her strengthening in all areas and personal and spiritual maturation (James 1:2).

Isaiah 61:1-4 describes Sheryl well. Her broken heart was bound up; she recognized how she was imprisoned and so proclaimed the freedom that was rightfully hers. Her grieving heart, which mourned for years, received the joy and oil of gladness. And so began the healing, which resulted in the transformation process of change and her becoming an oak of righteousness with the focus on glorifying God through it all. Sheryl has been repaired in and through Christ, and the devastations and destructions that the enemy has meant for evil are being rebuilt in her in strikingly divine ways (Gen 50:20).

As you read and travel along with Sheryl, I encourage you to consider the steps she has taken as possibilities for yourself because that is her ultimate purpose in writing this - for you to know the Hope within and to receive the benefit of healing, change and growth for yourself and for God to receive all the Glory!

Kelley Goodall, M.A., M.A.
Founder of Intentional Being

Introduction

When you have hit rock bottom, there is nowhere to go but up! Life can be full of tragedy, loss and sorrow, but there is no reason to allow it to define who you are or what your future will look like! John 10:10 states that, "the thief (devil) comes only to steal and kill and destroy; I (Jesus) have come that they (you and I) may have life and have it to the full." Ultimately, I have learned that we will have the life that we dwell on the most. Let me explain by quoting a couple more truths from God's Word: Matthew 12:34b, "For out of the abundance of the heart the mouth speaks." It only makes sense that we will eventually start to believe, think, speak and act like what we continually rehearse in our head, whether good or bad, truth or lies. That is why it is so very important to truly know God's Word inside and out. God's Word is the truth and it says in John 8:32 that if we know the truth, it will make/set us free! Also, it is good to remember that God is not a man that He should lie (Numbers 23:19). John 8:44b states that the devil has been "a murderer from the beginning, not holding to the truth, for there is no truth in him. When he lies, he speaks his native language, for he is a liar and the father of lies." So, my friends, we must be aware of who we allow to speak into our lives.

Those who are truly children of the King of Kings and Lord of Lords will not continue to speak negativity, slander, hatred, disrespect, false accusations, persecution and the like over, at or into our spirit/life. Galatians 5: 24-26, "Those who belong to Christ Jesus have crucified the flesh with its passions and desires. Since we live by the Spirit, let us keep in step with the Spirit. Let us not become conceited, provoking and envying each other." Ephesians 4:29, "Do not let any unwholesome talk come out of your mouths, but only what is helpful for building others up according to their needs, that it may benefit those who listen." My point here is to encourage you to truly be aware of your internal thoughts, external words and your actions at all times. Surround yourself with people who will speak life, encouragement and God's Word of truth into you. Stay constantly meditating on God's Word, so if falsehoods are spoken, you will pick up on them right away, rebuke them, cut them off and immediately speak God's Truth over yourself and into the situation. Let me tell you, God will honor your pursuit of His presence and His Word. He will take you into the secret place and begin revealing His heart and character to you, His beloved! Not only that, but Jesus will comfort, strengthen and restore every broken, empty, and painful place in your heart and life! Psalm 16:11 says that "in His presence, is the path of life and fullness of joy!"

From me to you, I am praying for each and everyone who takes hold of this book. Stay open to the still small voice of Holy Spirit as you read. Let the tears flow as you resonate with your own painful present or past of codependency, heartache, tragedy or the like. Pause to allow Holy Spirit to reveal areas of unforgiveness, bitterness, resentment, judgment, hatred towards other people, yourself, or even towards God. Repent and ask for Jesus to forgive you for your sins that were revealed. Thank Him for His finished work on the cross and for setting you free from all of these things that have been holding you back from moving forward into the dynamic future God has for you. Begin decreeing and speaking out the truth of God's Word over yourself, your current circumstances and over your future. Your life of codependent captivity will begin to transform into a life of favor-filled freedom in Jesus' Name! Live your new life continually in Jesus' presence and you will see that those things that the devil meant to harm you with, God will turn them all around for your good, and even save many lives in the process (Genesis 50:20)! Let this journey of transformation and new hope begin!

Chapter One:
The Beginning of the End

"TO EVERYTHING THERE IS A SEASON, AND A
TIME TO EVERY PURPOSE UNDER THE HEAVEN..."

ECCLESIASTES 3:1

Bliss to Unsettledness

August 8th, 2012, my much-anticipated wedding day arrived. Our pre-wedding party had been just a couple of days before in Nashville, TN. What should have been a fun and memorable time, ended up with us arguing and wondering why we were even together. That night should have been the final red flag that had me call the whole thing off, so we could go our separate ways. I thought that I was being "Christ-like" as I continued to forgive, make excuses for his behavior, and to love unconditionally, yet, what I would find out much later, was that I was living in denial, insecurity, poor boundaries and codependency.

Mason and I had only met three years prior and had even gone our separate ways for one and a half of those years. Through my persistent emails and phone calls, we had seemed to reconcile our differences and had decided to get back together. I remained a bit skeptical of a true change in behavior, but day after day, he seemed pretty consistent and much more light-hearted and open to prayer and to Bible study. I am one who always tries to see the very best in others. I can see not only potential, but God's gifting within people and do whatever I can to draw it out. I knew that this man was a good man, deep down, who had so many amazing gifts and talents from the Lord. Mason had experienced a very traumatic childhood and a few other setbacks in life that had definitely tainted his view of God, well-meaning people, and life in general. I guess that I thought that with my love, encouragement and God's help, we could redeem the painful past and have a beautiful marriage. Even though I wholeheartedly believe that this could have been our reality, eventually, it was far from what actually transpired.

We were married in August and then packed the moving truck with all of my belongings and we moved to his house in Minnesota. This was a very challenging move for me since I knew no one in his hometown and I had also heard how horribly cold the winters get there! I must say that I was right about this move being a bit challenging. I was trying to set some of my familiar things up in this large house, so it would feel more like it was our home together, but something just did not feel right. Mason genuinely loved me, and my family and I genuinely loved him and his children, so I knew that I should just give this new transition some time to settle and for us to find our new rhythm.

I suppose that we found our new rhythm, but it was to the beat of major dysfunction. We would dance two steps forward with love and forgiveness, and five steps backward with hateful, judgmental comments and false accusations. There always seemed to be some kind of underlying power struggle and unsettledness in our relationship from day one. I had grown up in a very loving, forgiving and strong Christian family, but my new husband had not. He grew up surrounded by physical, emotional and spiritual abuse, mainly coming from an alcoholic and non-faithful, non-present father. The thing is, I knew a lot of these circumstances going in to this relationship, yet chose to love him through them anyway. Even though love covers a multitude of sins (1 Peter 4:8), loving someone does not necessarily "fix" all of the trauma from the past. You can only give to someone else what you possess from within, good or bad, truth or falsehood, light or dark. Whatever you have to give, may or may not be received by the other person, as well. Relationships do not just evolve, they must be intentionally nurtured with consistent communication, forgiveness, giving and loving from the heart. The past, unfortunately, has a nasty habit of rearing its ugly head when you least expect it to. So many of our responses are actually negative reactions to former triggers that have not been properly repented of, completely severed and ultimately healed by the blood of Jesus. Mason and I were just two hurting, lonely people who were looking for love and hoping to redeem the time from our individual past of hurt and regret.

My husband's twenty-two-year-old son, David, would be living with us for awhile and his twelve year old daughter, Emily, would be with us a little less than half of the time. I fell in love with these two children right away, even though we went through a period of adjustments. There was also an older daughter, Sarah, and her husband who lived out of state. Sarah was very much against her dad remarrying and, would have nothing to do with either one of us, unfortunately. We were barely surviving the first month of our new marriage, when an unthinkable tragedy hit our household on September twenty eighth, 2012.

From Bad to Worse

I mentioned earlier that my twenty-two year old step son, David, was living with us. David was a handsome, intelligent, kind-hearted and fun-loving young man. He and his friends were devoted motorheads who were always working on a car or motorcycle out front in our garage. One night, he and his friend Ben went out late to test drive a car that they had just rebuilt the engine on. Shortly after midnight, we were awakened by our doorbell. Two policemen were at our door to inform us that David and Ben had been in a car accident and both boys had died at the scene. What, Lord?! We were still half asleep, I think, and in utter shock and disbelief at what we had just heard. Mason went to call his ex-wife, Kelly, and let her know the tragic news. I went directly in to prayer and to crying out to the Lord for answers. God promises to answer us when we call out to Him (Jeremiah 33:3). He actually did give me a couple of nuggets of truth to my questions, but also gave me a very clear Scripture to stand on: Psalm 102:28, "The children of Your servants shall dwell secure; their offspring shall be established before You." I knew right away that God was letting me know that even in the midst of this tragedy, David was alive and well in

Heaven with Him. This direct promise from God had given me an internal peace for sure.

The days that followed this tragedy were extremely difficult. There were so many mixed emotions and not much communication between Mason and I, as we now had an October funeral to prepare for. Even though David was not my biological son, because of my new union with Mason, my heart was deeply grieved. I had started to develop my own relationship with David and was growing very fond of him indeed. Needless to say, we made it, barely, through both of David and Ben's funerals. We were the walking wounded and truly numb to most everything else that was going on all around us. I tried my best to be there for Mason, but all he wanted from me was "patient quietness". With all of this "quietness", I felt like I had not only lost my stepson, but my new husband as well. We finally came to the conclusion that what Mason truly wanted and needed at this point, was some time alone to try and process all the painful emotions of David's death. What do I do now, Lord?

Some Time Apart

I packed up a few things and my little dog, and set out for Oklahoma. Wow, what a way to start off a new marriage; already separated one month later. I had no idea how long that we would be apart, so I moved in with my parents and even found a job, hairdressing at a local salon. I also had a lot of sleepless nights full of many tears and questions, so I started going to grief counseling once a week. My Christian counselor was Katy. I soon realized that God had definitely brought her and I together. She had such a wonderful, understanding and encouraging way about her that always made me feel like I was in a very safe place.

I didn't hear from Mason very much over the next few months, despite my persistence to stay in touch. So, disillusioned with his behavior, I continued to put a lot of hours in at the salon and even went back to beauty school to add a few more hours to become licensed in Minnesota. I stayed involved with my church family and in counseling as the months went by. By April, my husband had decided to come and drive back with me. I knew that I should go back with him, but the on-going, pent up depth of his anger, bitterness and control issues started to surface even before we left my parents' home. I knew that I had to trust the Lord and to lean hard into Him if I was ever to make it through the next few months.

TIMELY TAKE-A-WAYS

* I learned the importance of not ignoring any and all "red flags", (warning signs and/or lack of peace), when in a relationship. You should never feel like you are trying so hard to make it work. No! God will align the both of you in His perfect timing and with His peace if it is meant to be. Trust your "gut". As a born-again believer, I know that my "gut" is Holy Spirit giving me divine guidance.

* I learned how important it is to have a deep root system in truly knowing the goodness of God's character. Your daily intimate time with Jesus is of utmost importance! When tragedies come, then you will be ready to hold tightly to your anchor of God's goodness, no matter what storm of life blows your way. You will know that the tragedy is NOT from God, but that through it, He will never leave or forsake you.

Chapter 2:
Walking Through a Fog

"WHERE THERE IS NO COUNSEL, THE
PEOPLE FALL; BUT IN THE MULTITUDE OF
COUNSELORS THERE IS SAFETY."

PROVERBS 11:14

Hope Deferred

When we got back into town, I knew that it would be best to go and find a job and a local Christian counselor. The silence kept growing between Mason and I, and he refused to go to any type of counseling at all. When I did try to talk to him, it would almost always end up in a huge fight, so I just kept things rather "surfacy" in order to keep the peace.

By September 2013, one year after David and Ben's death, their friends wanted to have a get-together in our garage where they had all spent so much time together. We had a large barbecue and the kids had brought Chinese lanterns to light and set afloat in the boys' honor. The celebration of their life was very thoughtful and beautiful, until many of the kids, and even my husband, started drinking a little too much.

By this time, my hope of any lasting positive behavior and loving interactions between Mason and I was really waning. The drinking and emotional abuse continued to increase greatly, and my emotional and physical health started to decline. I thank God that He had placed an amazing Godly counselor, Debbie, in my life. She actually invited me and my little Chay Chay to stay in her finished basement as long as we needed to. I prayed a lot about her offer, and finally came to the conclusion that I needed to separate myself, for a time, from the toxic environment in our home. I also made sure that Mason knew that I loved him dearly, but what was going on between us was not ok, and this time, he really needed to get serious about finding some counseling. After all, we had sweet Emily's wellbeing to take into consideration as well. So, I moved a few things over to Debbie's, for yet our second separation in our short time of being married. While staying with Debbie, I paid her a little rent each month, continued on with my intense weekly counseling and nutritional therapy so I could regain my health again.

Digging Deeper

It was October of 2013 when I moved into Debbie's basement. Although brokenhearted and confused with everything, I felt an extreme peace there. I didn't know it at the time, but the next six months were about to be the most soul-searching and eye-opening months ever! I was still holding down a full-time job, working hard on healing my broken heart and on refining my character to reflect more of Jesus.

One thing that Holy Spirit revealed to me through intense counseling and in listening to His still small voice, was that I had been extremely codependent. What did that even mean, really? Webster's defines codependency as "an emotional and behavioral condition that affects an individual's ability to have a healthy, mutually satisfying relationship." Wikipedia describes it as "a dysfunctional helping relationship where one person supports or enables another person's addiction, poor mental health, immaturity, irresponsibility, or underachievement." Mental Health America states that this leaves the relationship basically "one-sided, emotionally destructive and/ or abusive." Wow, what a blow to my self-esteem! I thought that I was just being thoughtful, loving, selfless and gracious, but come to find out, I had really been adding to the dysfunction of my relationships. So, this troubling revelation was the beginning of my repentance for this behavior and to get to the bottom of why I was so prone to it. Now came the hard work of transforming and renewing my mind with what the Word of God said about me, not the enemy's lies. For the first time in my adult life, I was now learning to love, value, respect and set positive boundaries for myself. Thank You Jesus for not leaving me the way I was!

Debbie and I tried to encourage Mason to come for marriage counseling. He did come a couple of times, but wasn't agreeing with the material, so he stopped coming. By April 2014, I decided to move back home, due to Mason's request. By this time, I was getting much stronger spiritually and emotionally and had even been presented with two new job opportunities, which I took! I also kept myself busy teaching a little girl's Bible class every Wednesday evening at our church. Mason had started to come back to church, so we could go as a family again. He and David's friends had also been planning to have a special memorial event in September to honor David and Ben's memories. This "Motorhead Memorial" would be a yearly car show and fund-raising event for young, deserving motorheads to be able to go to mechanic's school. I loved the fact that Mason seemed to be thinking more positively and I actually started to feel a bit hopeful. I tried to remain supportive and helpful as Mason continued to process David's death. Most of the time, I was still left alone physically, emotionally and spiritually, but continued to press in to the hope that one day he would "let me in".

Tough Love

I continued to stay very busy with my jobs, school and other outings with Emily, and in leading a couple of different ministries at the church. I started spending even more time in God's Word, prayer and in worship as we had entered into the new year of 2015. Even though Mason had started to get more involved in church, unfortunately our marriage was growing more distant and abusive day after day. I knew in my spirit that I must just totally leave him and our marriage in God's hands and pursue all that He was passionately calling me into. I had laid so many of my own passions aside and had really lost who I was. I had been allowing grief, a toxic environment and unmet expectations to dictate my life, and I had decided that enough was enough! I immediately started a "Thankful Notebook" and made a point to write in it every day no matter what. I also got involved with the music ministry at church, my strong passion, and also was making plans to go with the pastor's wife and others on a mission trip to the Ukraine in September. Life was returning to me, and to top things off, the movie WAR ROOM came out in August. This movie made such a huge impact upon my prayer life, my hope of restoration of our marriage, and in understanding the power of decreeing God's Word over every situation in my life.

At the end of August, we all went to Branson, Missouri with my sister's family and my parents to celebrate my parent's fiftieth wedding anniversary. We did have some joy-filled times, but, unfortunately, most of them were filled with tension for Mason and I. When we returned home, I started packing for the ten day mission trip to the Ukraine. In spite of some massive spiritual warfare and debilitating nerve pain down from my neck into my right arm, before we went and while we were there, I had an incredible time of spiritual growth. I was filled with a bit more hope that maybe Mason would want to go to marriage counseling with me and work on our relationship. Unfortunately, my bubble burst when I was "welcomed home" with more distain and persecution.

The week after I got home was filled with final preparations for the Second Annual Motorhead Memorial. The fund-raiser had been another success, but I could tell that both of our hearts weren't in to it as much. By October, there was zero love or affection from Mason, and he still was not interested in any personal or marital counseling. Even though I was getting much stronger spiritually, I knew that if I was to keep moving forward in my emotional and physical healing, I had to make another tough decision, and soon. Proverbs 11:14 says that, "Where there is no guidance, a people falls, but in an abundance of counselors there is safety." So, I set off to get the wise counsel of my pastor and two other Christian counselors, along with my own seeking the Lords' wisdom for my next steps. I could feel my life spiraling downward in to deep depression no matter what I did to try to combat it. I literally felt like I was, at least partially, dying inside. It had been almost three years of promises to change and do better, and now I just wasn't believing him any longer. To complicate matters, one of my close family members had to be hospitalized, plus, the holidays and a harsh winter were on the way. With all of these factors and the Godly counsel I had received, I decided to make the "tough love" choice of separating by moving back to Oklahoma. I made sure that Mason knew that I still loved him and that I did not want a divorce, but that he needed to show me that he was serious this time about getting some major, ongoing personal and grief counseling for all that he'd been through in his life. I had finally built the courage to stand up for myself, end the abuse and control, set healthy boundaries, and to take care of my wellbeing. Major transitions have never been easy for me.

TIMELY TAKE-A-WAYS

*   I learned that life is not all about me and having every expectation met. I have truly learned how to better extend grace to others, especially when they are grieving. Everyone reacts to and processes pain differently. The key is to not judge others, but to extend grace, love and kindness to them.

*   I learned the importance of daily soul searching and to not be ashamed to get Godly, professional help if necessary. Before you go and point the finger, remember that four of those fingers are pointing right back at you! It is always best to work on your own character first, to get healthy and to grow, so you are in a better place to help others in need.

Chapter Three:
Painful Transitioning

"DO NOT BE CONFORMED TO THIS
WORLD, BUT BE TRANSFORMED BY THE
RENEWAL OF YOUR MIND…"

ROMANS 12:2

The Worst Day of My Life

I told Mason that we needed to have a serious talk about some things. So, I prayed before our "meeting", and then proceeded to share my heart. Needless to say, this announcement to move back to Oklahoma for awhile, did not go over well at all. Mason was filled with rage, hateful, hurtful comments, and refused to listen to my concerns and to my true intent behind this decision. I told him that I'd been trying to understand his pain, but the way he was handling it with me was not ok. If I could just see that he was serious about getting help and changing for the better, I would happily move back, and we could start brand new again; but not until then. I was advised to not leave anything precious in the house that I cared about, and I am glad I took that advice. I later found out that some things that I had left behind were thrown into the burn pile out back and destroyed.

My moving day came and I had about ten friends to help me load everything up. I was heartbroken, yet again due to leaving all of my new friends, ministries and jobs behind. So much pain and brokenness caused me to weep bitterly over the next thirteen hour trip to Oklahoma. What was I doing? Had I truly heard from the Lord and made the right decision? Would I be able to live with my decision even if he changed but never wanted me back? So many hard questions…

My parents found a cozy little duplex for Chay Chay and I, and we moved in right before Thanksgiving. I truly felt loved and valued by all of my relatives and friends who knew the truth of everything that had happened over the past three years. I must say, though, that I had a rough time getting through the holidays without being happily together with my husband and step daughter. I called Mason, on Thanksgiving and on Christmas, but he would hardly talk to me and it sounded like he had already given up on our marriage.

The Lord blessed me from November through part of January with not having to work. I knew that Jesus just wanted to spend exclusive time with me, so I could start the healing process all over again. I also made the choice to get weekly counseling from Katy, to attend Celebrate Recovery, a Christian-based twelve step program, and to spend massive amounts of time in God's amazing Word and in His healing presence. Little did I know that I would really need this strengthening time to prepare me for what was coming later in January.

Before I left Minnesota, I had met with a lawyer for some professional legal advice concerning my temporary move back to Oklahoma. The whole time that Mason and I were separated, I had sent occasional cards and even little meaningful gifts to him and to Emily. I wanted them to know that I wanted to stay connected and hopeful for our marital reconciliation and restoration of our new family at some point. Unfortunately, all of my attempts to love and to stay connected were met only with distain and a hardened heart. By late January, early February, the unthinkable happened. I was served divorce papers.

Pressing Through the Numbness

My prayers seemed like they were only hitting a brick wall, yet I continued to trust God for a miraculous change of heart for Mason. I also did a lot of soul searching and continuous asking Jesus to keep my heart free from any unforgiveness, bitterness or resentment. I knew that it was high time to stop feeling sorry for myself and to start moving forward in to rediscovering my true identity and destiny in Christ. One thing that I knew I needed to do was to find a job. I started working at a hair salon in town a few weeks later, and even became close friends with a couple of Christian stylists there. I had also been following Lana Vawser's prophetic ministry for a few years and saw that she had a conference coming to Texas in February of 2016. I made plans to go, and it was at this conference that God began to confirm my true identity and destiny of "Healing Prophetic Worship." At the time, I did not exactly know what that meant, but knew that Holy Spirit would lead me into the details of it in His perfect timing. I also received a great amount of inner healing as I soaked in the Lord's presence during the teaching of the Word and through the powerful worship. It was also during this time that my close family member was finally released from the hospital, praise God!

The next conference the Lord led me to was held at Chuck Pierce's Glory of Zion International. This was a wonderful Passover celebration weekend at the end of April. I had never experienced a large multicultural apostolic church such as this one. There were extensive prophetic truths spoken, Holy Spirit's weighty presence, and extreme joy flowing from that place that I felt like I was worshipping in Heaven itself! I felt right at home and knew that God had me on a major journey filled with healing and reprogramming for such a time as this! The devil had unfortunately used Mason and others to fill my head so full of lies, that I truly lost sight of how valuable I was to God and to others. He was awakening me to the unique calling upon my life, so I could make a powerfully positive impact upon the lives of those around me.

Revival Fire Falls

It was now June of 2016. I had found out about a revival that had started in San Diego, California at the end of January and was currently still going strong. I was very curious to see what it was all about, so I started tuning in to watch this Fire and Glory Outpouring over live stream six nights a week. The meetings were led by Jerame and Miranda Nelson, and worship mainly by Andrew Hopkins. Oh my goodness, was I ever blown away by the anointed worship and the explosive teaching! Holy Spirit's presence came so powerfully every single night as people were being healed, set free and saved from everything imaginable; and this was even happening over the live stream! I was even starting to experience a major shift in my own mind and heart. Holy Spirit was doing such a deep, inner work in me that I started being filled to overflow with extreme joy and boldness to witness and to pray for people that I encountered throughout the day. I was so very hungry for more of God and to experience His manifest presence in such a tangible way like this, that I started making plans to fly down there so I could soak in this anointing in person!

Needless to say, that during all of this wonderful healing that God was doing within me, I was also still experiencing deep moments of grieving over my upcoming mediation, and most likely, divorce. I knew beyond a shadow of a doubt that God was setting me up to go to San Diego before I had to drive all of the way to Minnesota in July to finalize our divorce.

I had never been to San Diego, so I excitedly booked my flight, hotel and car for a whole week. When I got there, right away God blessed me with a free upgrade, a fun sports car to drive! The first night in my hotel I was awakened around two in the morning by a small earthquake! I later found out that the quake happened right as prophet James Goll, one of the speakers for the weekend, landed! I knew right away that God was shaking things up for a reason and that He had incredible plans for me there! God even made sure that I got to go see the animals at the famous San Diego Zoo, have some relaxing beach time, ride the Coaster (a fast train), and even take a ferry ride across to Coronado Island! God knew that I needed these fun times along with the amazing "Presence-Saturated" atmosphere to ensure more healing, strengthening and restoration of my weary-wounded heart and mind. Oh, what an awesome God I serve!

TIMELY TAKE-A-WAYS

*   I learned that when going through the fire, that I must make sure to spend even more time in Jesus' presence and in God's Word. It is not wise to just keep yourself busy to numb the pain of what you are going through. You must deepen your walk with Jesus by investing more time in becoming like Him. In turn, He will fill you with His extraordinary peace!

*   I learned that I must choose to forgive, love and bless others, no matter what they are choosing to do to me. I must learn how to respond like Jesus would and not to react. I must not hold any bitterness or unforgiveness in my heart towards anyone, or I will be held accountable. Never give up hope or in trusting God for a miracle turnaround in your situation. (Please be advised: If you are in a hostile, physically or emotionally abusive situation, by NO means am I advocating that you remain in harm's way. Please get professional help in making sure that you and your children are safe and well taken care of.)

Chapter Four: Overcoming with God's Love

"DO NOT BE OVERCOME BY EVIL, BUT OVERCOME EVIL WITH GOOD."

ROMANS 12:21

Angels Do Exist!

Mid July had arrived, along with the day of setting off for Minnesota. The Lord had decided to wake me up with a profound knowledge of His presence that day. As I opened my eyes, there to the right of my bed, right in front of me was a large angel standing about nine feet tall! I believed in angels but had never seen one before this. I was very much taken back by his stately presence, as he was looking right at me! I couldn't really make out his face, but it is like I instantly knew that he was my guardian angel. This angel had been directly sent by God that morning to remind me of His faithfulness to never leave or forsake me, especially throughout this painful divorce process.

What an extreme blessing to have the love and support of my true family and friends through all of this. I left my sweet little Chay Chay in my good friend's care, loaded up my parent's van, and away we all went on the long journey to Minnesota. I was pretty quiet the whole time as I was praying and decreeing God's Word over our situation and over everyone involved.

The day of mediation came and though I was confident that God and His angels were right there with me, I was definitely nervous about seeing Mason again. Even after all of this, my heart was still believing for a miraculous reconciliation and a halt to this ridiculous mediation. Unfortunately, that was not even close to what was in Mason's heart. We had to briefly meet in the same room for a short set of instructions before we went to our separate rooms with our respective lawyer. I was so hoping to catch his eye for a glimmer of hope, but only broke my heart that he wouldn't even look at me.

What a horrible process the whole mediation was. We countered back and forth for awhile, but I quickly realized that Mason had no intention of leaving me anything, not even what was legally half. So, in order to keep us from having to go to court for more expense and heartache, I decided to settle on a small amount and to trust God to supernaturally make up the rest. The worst and most painful part of the whole mediation was that I was forced to agree to not contact Emily at all. If I did try to contact her, I could be fined or imprisoned for violating the restraining order. Wow, so harsh, hurtful and unnecessary for one who I'd come to love and care for as if she were my very own. Somehow, I knew that God would heal my heart from all of this and that I must forgive Mason and move on.

Rays of Hope

Life must go on after a divorce. I had spent the last two to three years of transitioning into being a new wife, step mom, friend, employee, and ministry leader in a brand new community away from anything or anyone familiar to me. Somehow, now, I had to transition yet again into being single, on limited funds and without knowledge of my true purpose. I knew that I must not let this tragic event define me or delay the life that God had always meant for me to live. I thank God for His extraordinary care for me during the next few lonely and vulnerable months. I continued going to counseling, working full time, daily meditating on God's Word, and nightly worshiping on live stream with the Fire and Glory Outpouring.

In August I was introduced to Dylan. I truly had no interest in meeting anyone at this point. My heart had just been broken and my world had fallen apart. One of my friends kept insisting, so I finally agreed to go to dinner with him. I must say that Dylan was a very handsome, kind, polite and fun man to be with. We seemed to have quite a bit in common, so we ended up becoming close friends very quickly. He lived and worked out of town about eighty percent of the time, but it was still nice to have a new male friend in my life.

By October, one of my clients approached me about a part-time nanny position for his five year old daughter, Kacie. I had nannied in the past for three other families and had really enjoyed it. I prayed a lot about it, worked the hours out with the salon and took this new opportunity to invest into a child's life. The ironic thing is that when I found out that her middle name was Emily, my former step-daughter's name, I wept and wept. I also found out that this family was attending the same church that I was. Wow, was God ever wrapping His loving arms around me! I could actually feel my hope rising day by day.

Stepping Into Destiny

The holidays came and went pretty quickly. I always do a twenty-one day fast in January to start out the New Year seeking the Lord's heart for me. So much had happened already, that I couldn't wait to see what all He had coming in 2017! One thing that I nor my family were planning on, is when my dad found out that his right retina was in the process of detaching. So, I became the designated driver, due to this serious procedure and follow up visits being done by a specialist in a larger city forty-five minutes from where we lived. The initial procedure went well and the healing process was underway. One week later I took him back for his check-up, and we were hit again with bad news. This time, there was a small hole that had appeared in yes, the same eye. So, he had to be rushed into an emergency surgery that very day. Needless to say, my parents and I were in tears. We had expected one thing but had received a completely other. Yet, our God was so very faithful over that long month of recovery, and I also had the privilege of driving, praying for dad and helping mom out with things as well.

The next thing I knew was finding out about Patricia King's Women on the Front lines Mentoring weekend coming to Oklahoma City in March. I had a stirring in my spirit that I needed to be there, so I registered for it. That powerful weekend sparked a deep calling into my destiny that I knew I had to answer to. I took some paperwork to fill out and to apply for acceptance into Patricia King's Women in Ministry network. I found out a couple of weeks later that I was accepted into this amazing company of Christian women. I also knew that I needed to be at the Women on the Frontlines World Convention in Phoenix, Arizona over my birthday weekend in May. God was sure busy setting up all these divine appointments for me; one right after another!

What an amazing forty-eighth birthday that I had there in Phoenix! I had never felt so loved and poured into in all of my life. I was making connection after connection of Kingdom-minded women who were already becoming my new friends. The worship was incredibly freeing and off the charts, as was the powerful Bible teachings, testimonies of God's goodness and healing power, and the prophetic prayer ministry. I definitely came away with my identity healed and empowered to start moving forward into more of my destiny calling.

Also, while attending the conference, I felt very led to align myself with Joan Hunter Ministries. I really resonated with her focus on healing the whole person; spiritually, physically, emotionally, relationally, and financially. Specifically, I knew that Holy Spirit was leading me to sign up for her healing school and then to apply for ordination through her ministry. I also saw a flyer at Joan's table that was encouraging others to sign up to go with her to The Holy Land of Israel. Oh, my how my wheels were turning now! I had always wanted to go to Israel, and what a better time than to go with Joan after I completed my ordination with her!

When I returned back home, I made the decision, well, I was more talked into it by my dentist, to start the whole Invisalign, braces for adults, procedure. My teeth had always been a bit of an embarrassment to me, but I had made it this far without straightening them, so why did I really need them? I gave in to the pressure of being told that I really did need them, so, even as I type, I have several more months to go before they are completely straight. It has been a grueling process, but hopefully I will think it has been worth it when it is all said and done.

The month of June brought on a serious surgical procedure for my sister Lisa, which God brought her through beautifully. By July, I was well into my healing school course studies and very busy with my jobs and deadlines. I had been sensing that God was getting ready to move me out of the current hair salon that I was in. Sure enough, not long after I had been feeling this way, a customer of mine told me about an immediate opening for a salon manager at a nearby retirement village. The ironic thing was that many years ago, right out of beauty school, I had worked at this same upscale retirement village. Wow, was it meant for me to be there again? I was called in for an interview and I had told them that I still wanted to be able to nanny for Kacie, if that would work for them. To my surprise, the management told me that I was definitely the one they wanted, and that they would agree to my terms and hours.

Talk about a whirlwind of events, emotions and upgrades! There were a lot of preparations and supplies to purchase and get set up for both salons, one in each building. What a wonderful opportunity to release God's love, encouragement, and healing prayer to these beautiful people. I made it through a very stressful month of leaving the former salon, setting up the two new salons, finishing up my schoolwork in preparation for ordination in September, and even starting to raise funds for the Israel trip in March of 2018. All of this extreme favor and acceleration was absolutely overwhelming, but so were the enemy's attacks upon me and even on my family members.

It seems that I have struggled with my digestive system for most of my adult life. I can usually control my flare ups with eliminating trigger foods and by consuming digestive enzymes, probiotics and aloe vera juice. It was only two days before my ordination weekend and I ended up in the ER for a couple of hours of tests. I was having a severe burning in my chest and difficulty in breathing deeply. I knew that, most likely, this attack was more spiritual in nature than even physical, but I went to the ER just in case. Come to find out, it was only severe inflammation in my esophagus, so I cursed the spirit of infirmity and declared that my body was completely healed and restored in the Name of Jesus! Nothing was going to stop me from going to my ordination and carrying out God's plans towards my destiny.

The weekend in Tomball, TX with Joan Hunter, her staff and all of my new like-minded friends was exactly where I knew that God wanted me. No wonder the devil had tried so hard to keep me away! When I got back home, the Lord had been speaking to me about letting my nanny job go. I had been getting so very busy at the salon and then going directly to take care of Kacie until seven or later in the evening. I knew that I physically, spiritually and emotionally could not keep up this pace much longer. So, by October, I was now working full time at both salons, and preparing for the busy holidays. I was heartbroken to end my season with Kacie, but I knew that God had allowed me to make an important impact upon her life over the past year, and now He had new adventures in mind!

TIMELY TAKE-A-WAYS

*   I learned to not allow the disappointing decisions in my past to define me. I cut off all word curses that others or even that I had spoken over myself, and only spoke life and abundance over my future. I began to decree and declare God's promises over every detail of my life.

*   I learned to get out of my comfort zone and to explore ways that I could serve and be a blessing to others. I really focused on re-discovering who God had created me to be and all that He had gifted me in and destined me for. I began to start expecting miracles and divine appointments as I moved forward with peace and excitement for my future!

Chapter Five: A Year of New Beginnings

"Forget the former things; do not dwell on the past. See, I am doing a new thing!"

Isaiah 43: 18-19a

The Trip of a Lifetime!

Somehow, by God's amazing grace, I had made it through the busy holidays. God was really blessing me with extreme favor financially and with more flexibility in this new position. I also had ended up raising a little over half of my funds needed for the Israel Healing for the Holy Land Tour coming up in March. The Lord was already working out all of the details for me, so I could be in Israel for two whole weeks! My parents had agreed to dog sit for their "grand dog" Chay Chay, and a wonderful friend of mine had agreed to keep both salons running smoothly for me as well.

Between some health issues, and even a little health scare with Chay Chay a few days before I was to leave for Israel, the devil was sure working overtime to keep me worried and discouraged. God was so very faithful to assure me that He had everything and everyone of my concerns already taken care of. Due to all of my faithful prayer warriors, God's angelic assistance, and in decreeing God's Word over my situation, I had made it to the airport to begin my long journey to Israel.

Twenty-some hours and several security checks later, I finally arrived in beloved Israel! I had traveled all the way by myself, but excitedly met up with around fifty other people who had signed up for this tour with Joan Hunter Ministries like I had. Along with Joan, her husband Kelly, their photographer and videographer, was also a professional Israeli tour guide that they had hired. This man was literally a walking encyclopedia and he enriched our experience greatly. So, between the amazing Israeli food, the new friendships I was making, the beautiful land of incredible historical sights, and the powerful way that it made the Bible come alive, I can wholeheartedly say that this truly was the trip of a lifetime!

I must indulge in a few highlights from our trip. It may be hard to list just a few, but I will try! Everywhere that we sat foot where Jesus had performed miracles, actually radiated with His presence. I was most impacted by our boat ride across the Sea of Galilee, where Jesus had walked on the water. As we were worshipping, I felt like Jesus asked me, "Sheryl, if I called you out like I did Peter, would you come to Me? Wherever I call you, will you go?" Wow, was that an experience that I will never forget! The next powerful experience was being baptized in the Jordan River. I will never forget it for two reasons; the first being that it was literally ice cold and my whole body from my waist down was totally numb! The second reason is that the Lord had spoken to me the day before, that He would "wake me up from out of the water". I asked Him what He meant by that and He spoke again; "I will wake you up to My wisdom and revelation into where and what I am leading you next." Wow, confirmation indeed!

It seemed like each stop we made just kept building in intensity upon the last. When we set foot in Shiloh, I knew it was going to be powerful. As we walked over the rich ground full of olive trees, I was literally overcome with great expectation for miracles. Joan Hunter anointed all of our hands with the Shiloh olive oil and commissioned us into the "more of God"! Holy Spirit began to speak to me so very clearly about some details about my calling and oh how my excitement was building! Our next stop was Jerusalem and the Garden Tomb. This garden was such a beautiful and serene place. We all took communion in the garden and worshiped there, how powerful! When I stepped into the tomb where Jesus had been buried for three days, but then rose again, I could feel the electricity in the walls! I immediately started to tear up, due to my sorrow of those who crucified Him and put Him in the tomb; but also due to my joy, as I remembered His great sacrifice and love for me. The inscription on the inside of the door reads, "For He is not here; He has risen!" Amen and Amen! Well, I could literally go on and on about the Western Wall, the Pools of Bethesda, The Upper Room, the Dead Sea and more; but perhaps that should be in a book all of its own!

Give Thanks in All Things

I found it very hard to leave Israel. We were constantly on the go and got to experience so much, but there was oh so much more. All of the hours of walking and stair climbing for nine days and now sitting for twenty-four more hours in a plane, was very grueling on my body, to say the least. I have been challenged with some spinal, muscle and vascular issues for much of my adult life. I suppose that standing for thirty-one years as a hairdresser has not done my body any favors as well! Nevertheless, I made it back home to rest for a day or two, and then back to work I went. God was so very good to sustain me with His strength and joy as I got back into the swing of things at work. I missed Israel terribly, but was very happy to see my family and my little Chay Chay, as I had made it home safely!

I knew that my dad had four surgeries scheduled (all in one day!), for the month after I returned home from Israel. I truly thank the Lord that I was able to help mom and dad out during that time, as the healing process took much longer than expected. So, April and May were very busy months for me as I worked a full day and then went right over to my parent's house to help out there. Somehow in all of the business of life, I managed to get one year older as well!

When June rolled around, I had signed up to go to Rick Pino's Heart of David "Presence" conference weekend in Austin, Texas. I was first introduced to Rick's worship music at Patricia King's Women on the Frontline World Convention just a year prior. I had really enjoyed his refreshing style and uncanny way of ushering in Holy Spirit's presence. This conference was literally off the charts for me, as it filled me with such deep joy and confirmation of my calling into "healing prophetic worship". It is so deeply refreshing to truly know who you are and what you were created for! I give God all of the credit for the different prophetic voices that He has used to speak so profoundly into my life; especially over the last few years. Many of these wise, prophetic and/or apostolic voices, have been introduced to me through the Elijahlist, online daily emails from many trusted prophetic voices around the globe. One apostle that I really resonated with, was Apostle Joe Joe Dawson, out of Texarkana, Texas. I contacted him and made arrangements to meet up with him and his wife Autumn, and to attend ROAR church in mid August. I had no idea what God had in store for me, but I had been hearing "Texas" in my spirit for a couple of years; so, I knew that God was definitely up to something good!

The Adventure Has Only Just Begun!

The drive to Texarkana was absolutely beautiful. I felt like I needed to remain quiet and expectant to hear Holy Spirit speak to me the whole way there. In meeting with the Dawson's and in experiencing the amazing prophetic worship and teaching, I knew that I was amongst like-minded, Kingdom people. The more we talked and got to know each other, I was encouraged and welcomed to become a member of the ROAR Apostolic Network. I knew that this was where the Lord was leading me, and I also knew that I needed to come back in September for the commissioning service with Ken Malone and Dutch Sheets. I really did not know what "commissioned" even meant, so I looked it up! Dictionary.com defines commission as "the act of committing or entrusting a person, group, etc., with supervisory power or authority; authority granted for a particular action or function; the condition of being placed under special authoritative responsibility or charge; official assignment." Wow, what an honor to be entrusted into a Kingdom-minded, apostolic network of people, who are committed to the awakening, revival and reformation of cities, regions and nations!

God made sure that I had one major experience coming on the heel of another! I knew that I had the Head of the Year Conference at Chuck Pierce's Glory of Zion International Church coming up from September sixth through the ninth. That weekend was meant to celebrate the Jewish New Year of the Hebraic calendar, Rosh Hashanah (a time of personal, inner renewal and reflection). This conference was definitely the catalyst for launching me into my next season of destiny. When I got to my hotel room that evening, the number was 321; and the Lord immediately said to me, "Three, two, one, blastoff!". I knew exactly that He was confirming my question whether or not to move to Texarkana and to invest my life into ROAR apostolic church. Each service that I attended continued to point me closer to being involved in an apostolic revival hub and training center. I even met a lady that weekend at GZI who spoke into my life, that I would be shifting and moving sooner than I thought I would, so I had better start packing! What an awesome God that we truly have! He promises to show us "great and mighty things that we do not know" (Jeremiah 33:3), if we only ask Him. He loves it when we seek His heart on a matter, for He wants us to be in the center of His will even more than we want to be.

Well, let me just say that my commissioning service at ROAR church was an absolutely amazing confirmation of my calling for this season of life! I don't know if I have ever heard Holy Spirit speak louder and with more accuracy, even in multiple confirming words, than at this point in my life. The conference ended on September sixteenth, rather significant timing again, due to Yom Kippur. Yom Kippur is the Jewish Day of Atonement; a holy day of introspection and repentance, that begins at sundown on September eighteenth and goes into the evening of the nineteenth. The Lord surprised me with an amazingly clear and powerful dream/vision of further confirmation of my calling, and then woke me up at exactly three thirty-three (Jeremiah 33:3), on the morning of Yom Kippur. If you have not noticed yet, the Lord tends to speak to me through numbers. I see a lot of doubles, triples, quadruples and many numbers in sequence. Some numbers refer to Scripture verses that He is speaking to me about, but if I am in doubt, I will just ask Him what He wants me to know, and He will tell me! I will not reveal all of my "Holy Spirit download", but I will say that I now know, that I know, that I know,

I will be moving to Texarkana, Texas right after the holidays to begin my new adventure there at ROAR apostolic church. God has revealed some incredibly exciting details about walking in the fullness of my destiny there. I can hardly wait to move forward and experience all of what God has in store for me and for those whom I will run with in this strategic new era in time! Oh, how I give God all of the praise and glory for such a significant turnaround from a life of codependent captivity, into a favor-filled future, for such a time as this!!

TIMELY TAKE-A-WAYS

*   I learned how to look through the eyes of Jesus at my situation. When you are sold out to Jesus and to pleasing Him, you realize that there are really no setbacks in life, only "set ups". Within every situation you go through, Jesus sets you up for future advancements and for "leveling up". I learned to make the right choices in growing instead of becoming bitter.

*   I learned that with God ALL things are possible! God is limitless and longs to bless His children, especially when they are faithfully following Him in radical obedience. I have also learned to stay thankful in and through all things, because God will never leave or forsake me! I now daily expect to experience miracles and to be vitally used to bring hope, healing, revival and reformation to my city, nation and world! Praise God!

Chapter 6:
Embracing the Future

"You will make known to me the path of life; In Your presence is fullness of joy..."

Psalm 16:11

Limitless Adventures Await

Life is meant to be an exciting, character-enriching adventure. Yes, life is full of many ups and downs, but it is ultimately up to what you make of it. I believe that our attitude is of utmost importance when we journey through the wins and losses of this life. Actually, when you ask Jesus to forgive you of your sins and to become your Savior and Lord, there really are no losses, only learning experiences that are meant to transform us into the image of our Creator. Romans 8:28-29a says, "And we know that in all things God works for the good of those who love Him, who have been called according to His purpose. For those God foreknew He also predestined to be conformed to the image of His Son (Jesus)."

There is no reason to allow your present or past mistakes and trauma continue to define you. These events happened, so use them to learn, heal and grow from, and then be determined to move forward into all of the fullness that God has for you. Your past becomes a testimony to help encourage others and to give them hope by sharing all that you have learned from God and how He has miraculously brought you through! You must remember that you are never alone in your situation, and that there is always hope. How can you become better through what you are or have experienced, and not become bitter? Number one on your priority list must be to spend quality time in God's Word and in His presence. Romans 12: 1-2, "…I encourage you to surrender yourselves to God to be His sacred, living sacrifices. And live in holiness, experiencing all that delights His heart. For this becomes your genuine expression of worship. Stop imitating the ideals and opinions of the culture around you, but be inwardly transformed by the Holy Spirit through a total reformation of how you think. This will empower you to discern God's will as you live a beautiful life, satisfying and perfect in His eyes." These verses sum it up. There is NO substitution for spending quality time soaking in God's Word and in His presence. This, my friends, is exactly how I got through and came out of all of the darkness that I endured in those first three to four years of marriage. I also surrounded myself with Godly counselors and friendships who would intercede for me, speak the truth and stand beside me no matter what. You have got this, because God has got you in the very palm of His strong hands! Let go of the control and allow Him to work on your behalf and in His perfect timing.

Bless and Do Not Curse

I want to make something abundantly clear. I truly loved my husband and always knew that he was a good man. I believed in him and tried to support, encourage and honor him the very best that I knew how. I could not save or transform him, however, that was Jesus' responsibility. This book is in no way meant to expose, shame or to pass judgment upon him, either. I have written this book more so, as a testimony of one, me, who was ignorant of the harmful effects of codependency, enabling behavior, compromise and a lack of healthy boundaries. I have also written this book to help others to be aware of their intrinsic value and worth in God's eyes, and to never compromise or settle for less than God's very best for them in every area of their life. I believe that God will break through and do extraordinary miracles in the lives of those who choose to bless and not to curse; for those who choose to be courageous in getting wise, Godly counsel for the hurts and hang-ups in their lives; for those who choose to praise and worship God in the midst of their dark circumstances; for those who choose to obey God even when it is hard; for those who choose to trust in God's Word and not in their feelings or in their circumstances, and for those who choose to follow God's destiny for their lives, no matter the cost! Romans 12:14; 17-19, "Speak blessing, not cursing, over those who reject and persecute you. Never hold a grudge or try to get even but plan your life around the most noble way to benefit others. Do your best to live at peace with all people. Beloved, don't be obsessed with taking revenge, but leave that to God's righteous justice."

Three Main Keys to Focus On

1. Worship God in Spirit and in Truth (John 4:23-24)- Unashamedly praise, honor and adore Creator and Father God for who He is; Continually soak in Jesus' presence and in the truth and wisdom of God's Word in order to truly KNOW Him

2. Live a Loving, Holy and Surrendered Lifestyle (1 Peter 1:14-16) Radical obedience and unswerving devotion to the King of Kings and Lord of Lords; Having a clean and honorable character that always reflects Jesus and loves all people as He does

3. Decree and Declare God's Word with Bold Authority (Job 22:28)-Knowing Whose you are and who you are in Christ...Holy Spirit lives powerfully inside of you, so act like it! Live out your destiny carrying Jesus' healing, salvation, equipping/discipleship, revival and reformation to all people everywhere you go

Dare to Dream Again

Trust me, the pain and heartache will not last forever. Always hold on to hope. Give yourself some grace as you take time to heal from the traumas in your life and to move towards your exciting new future just up ahead. God promises that He has a hope and a prosperous future for you (Jeremiah 29:11); in fact, one that is immeasurably more than all you could ever ask or imagine that it could be! (Ephesians 3:20). The more quality time that you spend in Jesus' presence, He promises to reveal His heart and secrets to you (Jeremiah 33:3). He will also fill you with so much joy, love, peace and hope, that you will not be able to contain it; and you will not want to! You are NOT a helpless victim, you are a mighty victor in Christ Jesus, and no weapon formed against you will prosper (Isaiah 54:17)! What the enemy meant for your destruction, God has promised to bring good out of it, not only for you, but for others who hear your testimony (Genesis 50:20)! How powerfully exciting is that?! So, keep pressing onward and upward, my friend. Encourage yourself in the Lord along the way (1 Samuel 30:6) and refuse to get discouraged. Life is all about a growing and maturing process, so we can more beautifully reflect our Lord and Savior Jesus Christ. Others that know all that you have been through, will see you radiate with His countenance day after day with no "rational" reason why. This, my friend, is the golden opportunity to share your personal testimony of all that God has done and has brought you through. Others lives will be utterly changed and transformed as Holy Spirit speaks and works through you, and all for the wonderful glory and honor of Almighty God! This is your time, my friend, to finally break free from all codependent captivity and pain, and to start journeying into God's favor-filled freedom for your destiny! You can do all things through Christ who gives you strength (Philippians 4:13)! For such a time as this!

PRAYERS

Prayer Of Forgiveness For All Codependent Behavior:

"Dear Jesus, I ask You to forgive me for my codependent, controlling, insecure and/or less than Your best behavior for me. I thank You for renewing my mind so that I believe what You say about me. I don't have to compromise or settle in any area of my life because You have created me for extraordinary adventures and for Godly, respectful and loving relationships. Thank You for healing my heart from all of the pain and trauma in my life. I thank You that You are redeeming everything the enemy has destroyed, stolen or delayed in my life. From this day forward I choose to serve You and move forward in freedom from all codependent behavior. In Jesus name, Amen."

Prayer Of Salvation From Sin:

"Dear Jesus, I admit that I am a sinner (Romans 3:23; Romans 6:23).
I have done many things that don't please You. I have lived my life for myself and not for You. I am sorry for my rebellion and completely turn away from all sinful/wrong behavior and ask You to forgive me (Romans 10:9-10; 1 John 1:9). I believe that You died on the cross to save me from being eternally separated from You. You did what I could not do for myself and I am forever grateful. I ask You to take complete control of my life as I now call You Lord (Psalm 25). May I live every day in a way that pleases You. Thank You for loving and valuing me like no one else can (Romans 8:38-39). I know that You rose from death after three days, and because You live, I know that I will live with You forever in Eternity (John 3:16). Thank You for saving me. In Jesus Name, Amen."

ABOUT THE AUTHOR

SHERYL M. KRAFT was born and raised in a loving family of four, in Bartlesville, Oklahoma. She has been a licensed cosmetologist since 1987 and has lived in five other states and is working on moving to her sixth! Sheryl is an adventurer, and is very mission minded, as she has been to eighteen different countries/nations. She has a huge passion to see all people healed and whole in every area of their life, through the powerful and loving message of the Gospel of Jesus Christ! Sheryl flows in healing prophetic worship and powerful decrees from God's Word. She is called to equip God's people to be ready for world-wide outpouring of Holy Spirit, awakening, revival, and reformation of lives, cities, regions and nations for the End Time Harvest of souls. Sheryl is the founder of Warrior Reflections of You and is the creator of "It's Mirror Time!" Cards. Both ministries focus on the importance of knowing and using one's spiritual authority to boldly decree and declare God's Word in every situation.

As of 2017-Present, Sheryl is aligned and in good standing with the following apostolic ministries: Patricia King's Women in Ministry Network; Ordained through Joan Hunter's Healing Ministries; Commissioned Member of ROAR Apostolic Network (Apostle Joe Joe Dawson).

SHERYL M. KRAFT is the founder of Warrior Reflections of You and the creator of "It's Mirror Time!" Cards. Sheryl flows in healing prophetic worship and powerful decrees from God's Word, to bring Jesus' hope and freedom to people everywhere she goes. Sheryl's passion is to see every believer healed, fully equipped and walking in bold, Kingdom authority for world-wide revival and reformation.

CONNECT WITH SHERYL

Facebook: @skstormingthedarkness
Instagram & Twitter: @sksings4jc
Email: sksings4jc@yahoo.com

ABOUT WARRIOR REFLECTIONS OF YOU

In 2016, Warrior Reflections of You was founded by Sheryl M. Kraft to help encourage and equip God's people with the necessary tools to become spiritually and emotionally whole and empowered to spread the Gospel of Jesus Christ to every tribe, tongue and nation. Sheryl's specific passions are in two main areas: flowing in healing prophetic worship, and training God's people to become powerful prayer warriors who boldly decree and declare the Word of God over any person, situation or nation, for complete healing, awakening, revival and reformation to take place. Sheryl also places a strong emphasis on truly knowing Jesus, holiness, discipleship, hope, joy and lifestyle evangelism. Warrior Reflections of You is all about equipping the warrior bride of Christ (His Church/His people), to boldly reflect Jesus' character in every area of their life.

In Loving Memory

I would like to dedicate this first book to my former step son, David. I hate that your life was cut so short, but I look forward to seeing you in Heaven one day! I also dedicate this book to my former step daughter, Emily. I love and miss you more than words can say and will forever treasure our wonderful memories together.